candle details

RYLAND
PETERS
& SMALL
London New York

candle details

emily chalmers

photography by david brittain

Designer **Catherine Randy**
Senior editor **Sophie Bevan**
Location research **Emily Chalmers, Sarah Hepworth**
Production **Patricia Harrington, Gavin Bradshaw**
Art director **Gabriella Le Grazie**
Publishing director **Alison Starling**

Stylist **Emily Chalmers**

WARNING
Never leave a candle burning unattended. The author and publisher
accept no responsibility for any injury or misdemeanour resulting
from the application of information contained within this book.

First published in the USA in 2001 by
Ryland Peters & Small, Inc.
519 Broadway, 5th Floor
New York NY 10012
info@rylandpeters.com
www.rylandpeters.com

1 3 5 7 9 10 8 6 4 2

ISBN 1 84172 204 9

Printed and bound in China

contents

RIGHT: Mix classic and contemporary ideas. There is nothing more pure than fresh green leaves, smooth white pebbles, and clear water. Add a floating candle, and this table decoration will come to life. OPPOSITE: An example of unconventional candleholders. These sake bottles make excellent homes for long white tapers and, as each guest finishes their drink, another candle can be lit!

introduction

Candles have always been around the home for either practical or decorative use. They may be basic lighting "tools," such as votive candles, brought out in power outages, or specialized scented varieties lit to enjoy an aromatherapy experience. The word "candle" opens up a whole world of choice and variety, but it is the way they are displayed—however simple—that gives atmosphere to your home, be it outside lighting a garden path, at the dining table, or simply dotted around the house on window ledges and mantelpieces.

This book aims to inform and inspire, showing how candles can be used in the home and outdoors both for special occasions and everyday opportunities.

elements

FOR ILLUMINATION

The choice of candles available is endless, from tall thin tapers to chunky altar candles, tiny floating lights to towering flares. Candleholders, too, come in every shape and style, be it a sophisticated and beautiful candelabra or a humble old glass beaker. The possibilities are endless, and the selection can seem daunting. But, by choosing the right candles and presenting them successfully, you will immediately bring a magical feel to any setting.

candles

Good-quality candles burn well and last for hours. Try to keep the wicks to ¼ inch long and burn them away from drafts for the best performance.

Basic altar candles usually burn slowly, as do traditional pure beeswax ones—but watch the rolled beeswax variety, which burn down very quickly.

Most candles are naturally ivory in color, but there are plenty of painted or colored styles available. Beware of painted candles that have only a colored layer around the outside and burn to reveal white wax.

OPPOSITE LEFT: A good-quality altar candle wrapped in a large leaf and tied with string makes a stylish gift. Placed out of any drafts, it will burn for hours.

OPPOSITE RIGHT: Sheets of beeswax carrying a delicate imprint are rolled around a central wick to create candles of varying thicknesses.

LEFT: This candle has been dyed, painted, and molded to resemble a thick stalk of bamboo.

Why not extend your chosen color themes through to the candles you use to decorate for a special occasion? Also consider the textures that you go for—candles come in a variety of finishes, and some even have imprinted patterns on the outside. Standard "candlestick size" dinner candles come in almost every color, so collect a few options for different color schemes or burn a range of colors together for an eclectic feel.

BELOW LEFT: This interesting candle has been made from two layers of wax, and the outside has been given a rough chalky finish.

confident color and tempting texture

OPPOSITE RIGHT: A satisfying box of creamy white spherical candles—they would look good in a group burning on a pastel-colored plate.

THIS PAGE: These pastel standard-size dinner candles have a lovely, waxy feel. The wicks are still uncut, and each pair is joined in the traditional way.

ABOVE: These candles resemble pebbles
and come packaged on a bed of straw.
You can also find candleholders made from
real pebbles in all shapes and sizes to hold
a range of different-sized candles.

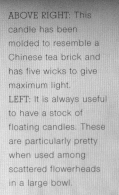

ABOVE RIGHT: This
candle has been
molded to resemble a
Chinese tea brick and
has five wicks to give
maximum light.
LEFT: It is always useful
to have a stock of
floating candles. These
are particularly pretty
when used among
scattered flowerheads
in a large bowl.

the natural look

Natural and neutral is a popular style in the modern home,
and this trend can be seen in candle design. In addition
to pure beeswax varieties, candles can be painted, dyed,
molded, and carved to resemble other natural materials.
You can find candles looking like pieces of bamboo,
wood, slate, or stone. Combine them with holders made
from rough and raw materials for a truly natural feel.

It is also handy to invest in a couple of large neutral
three- or four-wick pillar candles—they make good
centerpieces and generally give out a very warm light.

RIGHT: These delicate thin taper candles are very beautiful, but will burn quickly. Invest in a large supply and keep topping it up. You can buy individual taper holders, but be innovative. These candles will look stylish standing in small recycled glass bottles or even in pieces of fruit, such as apples, with a hole drilled in one side.

white light

White candles are classics and sit well in today's minimal environments. Try standing a bunch of fine long white tapers in a tall glass jar of coarse white salt, or sit some thick white altar candles in a tray of white pebbles collected on the beach or in white gravel from a garden supplier. Groups of tiny white votives look good along window ledges or sitting in clusters in little glass containers. Because of their metal cases, it is not necessary to use holders, so they are perfect to pop into unusual vases or beakers. And there is nothing more classic and elegant than tall, pure-white candles standing in shiny silver candlesticks at a formally laid table.

Votive candles are a good basic and, depending on their quality, can burn for many hours. They are relatively cheap and look best in multiples, either in lines or groups, around the home.

So long as it's safe, anything can be used as a candleholder. The whole aim is to burn candles safely while spreading light or creating an interesting decorative glow.

There are many styles of holders available, ranging from traditional candelabra and candlesticks to stands for thick altar candles and trays for multiple votives. The most interesting holders are often those improvised at home, such as a large glass brick on which to stand a thick, multiwicked candle, or an old vase that will cast an interesting pattern on the wall when lit internally with a votive.

REUSE AND RECYCLE
holders

OPPOSITE: The paper around this glass holder will create a soft glow, while the decoration gives an interesting Eastern look. THIS PAGE: These candleholders have all been made from cement to give a rough, heavy feel. For longer burning time, the votives could be replaced with altar candles of the same diameter. Here the candles sit in the fireplace to offer a welcoming glow.

RIGHT: These French garlic jars are lit internally with votives while the decorative cutout flower shapes throw interesting patterns onto the surrounding walls.

BELOW: Colorful bags are lit with candles sitting on a bed of sand and look very effective placed outdoors, either to light a pathway for an entrance or just to have dotted around at an evening garden party.

FAR RIGHT: A little glazed clay pot now houses a candle and can be reused again and again.

One of the joys of recycling found objects as candleholders is that it allows you to be colorful and innovative. Candles can be placed in colored glass beakers and bowls, bright fabric-covered pots—even inside paper bags. Candle bags can be bought specifically for outdoor lighting, but any paper bag can hold a candle as long as the flame is kept well away from the sides. If in doubt, place a glass jar inside the bag and put the candle in the jar. Floating candles will light up a colorful vessel, too. Newly available are colored wax bowls—they give a beautiful glow with the introduction of a simple floating flame.

bold colors, bright ideas

clear and simple

BELOW: These granitelike holders are made from concrete and have a fantastic unfinished look where they were broken from the mold.
RIGHT: Oyster shells have been collected from the beach and filled with candle gel around a central wick to create unusual lights for the table.

Because candles are a relatively natural means of creating light, holders created from natural materials or that simulate natural materials often seem appropriate. On this popular recycling theme, it is easy to see everyday objects transformed, such as paper cups or empty shells. Votives will sit happily in almost any safe canister, and candle gel is perfect for awkward shapes, such as oyster shells.

THIS PAGE: Paper cups double as stylish minimal candleholders—a very inexpensive way to decorate a room with soft light. Make sure the flame is kept well away from the beaker sides, and secure the candle inside so it won't move if accidentally nudged.

THIS PAGE: These little bottles are ideal for long taper candles and look good grouped on a brushed-steel tray ready to be offered to each guest around a table setting.

LEFT: A host of kitchen implements can be used as candleholders. The circular punched holes of a flatware drainer will cast an interesting pattern around the room. A simple but shiny cheese grater would also be effective.

perfect reflection

Because of their reflective surfaces, glass and metal are great materials as candleholders. Extend the idea of the candle in a wine bottle and recycle individual soda bottles to put at each place setting at a table. There are many metal items around the kitchen that will make interesting holders, and anything with a punched surface for grating or airing will cast a lovely pattern when it is lit by a candle. Make sure containers are clean and shiny—keep glassware sparkling bright with the occasional soak in diluted vinegar—and ensure naked flames are well away from surfaces that could be dangerous when hot.

candles

IN THE HOME

Candles make any occasion special, be it a mealtime, a party, or simply when you feel like unwinding. The effect of their light can be practical, relaxing, or festive, depending on how and where they are displayed. Utilize any suitable surfaces: window ledges, mantelpieces, and dining tables are obvious choices; but why not clear a shelf of your bookcase to display a line of colored votives or even use the bath rack to hold a special aromatherapy candle while you relax in a deep bath?

Incorporating candles into everyday activities is fun—imagine a garden room softly lit as daylight turns to dusk, or candles at the table for a relaxed family meal.

Don't wait for a special occasion to bring out the candles. Instead, make sure you always have a good supply on hand to choose from and you will never be without a candle—however humble—to suit the moment. Invest in a stock of candle "basics." Votives are always useful and can be easily popped into one-off containers. Altar candles are also reliable classics and will enhance any holder you use.

DECORATING WITH CANDLES
everyday

A garden room takes on a summery feel with fresh shades of lilac and lime. The storm lanterns are wrapped in banana-straw fabric that will diffuse the glow of the flames. Any sheer or loosely woven fabric is ideal—burlap, linen, or organdy, for example. Simply wrap the fabric around the lantern and join with a few long stitches. Finish the look with a simple table runner made from a coordinating fabric.

RIGHT: Remember that lanterns are not only for use outdoors. A basic square glass lantern hanging from an internal ceiling beam replaces overhead lighting. A few pebbles gathered from the beach are clustered around the flame, adding a vacation feel.

ABOVE: Scour second-hand stores for candleholders. An old glass brick provides the perfect holder for this square candle.

everyday objects transformed into extraordinary displays

Keep an eye out in second-hand stores and at garage sales—you will be surprised how many unusual or unwanted objects can become good homes for candles.

Search for colored antique cut-glass wine goblets that will bring an air of decadence to a display, or use old mixing bowls to float candles in colored water for a party. Kitchen glassware is often heatproof and very durable—ideal next to a naked flame. Lanterns—even jars and

BELOW: These heavy-duty glass containers from the kitchen have been filled with terracotta baking beans to support standard white candles.

TRANSFORM THE ORDINARY
TO CREATE A DAZZLING AND
INNOVATIVE SHOW OF LIGHT

glasses used as storm lanterns—are great for everyday use. They are perfect for outdoors or indoors, for table-top or floor-standing lighting, and the glass sides also provide a degree of safety at candlelit social gatherings. Experiment with wrapping the outer glass with colored plastic film, paper, or fabric to create an exotic rainbow glow that coordinates with other decorative effects in the room.

For a subtle, everyday look, pick holders made from natural materials, such as wood, stone, or metal. The rough texture of materials such as cement and terracotta also lends itself well to this look.

Anything candle-sized can be a candleholder—these old kitchen weights are great for different widths of altar candle, or they can be stacked to create a taller candlestick.

when more is more

Decorating with candles in multiples can be very effective, as well as practical from a lighting point of view. Tapers and votives are ideal since they are relatively cheap and look good in numbers.

Use long surfaces, such as spare shelves or ledges, to hold lines of candles. Try filling a large tray or shallow dish with votives to give a concentrated light source—perfect as a table centerpiece. Fill dishes with white or colored sand, salt, or pebbles to support groups of tapers, and experiment with forming lines of different groups for maximum effect. Light up the garden with multiple lanterns hanging from a single tree, or use a line of crooks—each holding a lantern—to illuminate a pathway.

BELOW LEFT: These tapers are supported by a mound of glass gravel in a bowl made from the shell of a coconut. BELOW RIGHT: An exposed wooden beam carries a row of little glass votives to light the stairway.

THIS PAGE: These inexpensive pots have been made from recycled glass and are perfect containers for little votives. Used either dotted around individually or in lines along the window ledges, they will add a warm welcoming touch to the room.

relaxing

Relaxing with candles is all about subtle scents and soft lighting. Look out for interesting ways to scent your rooms, using flower petals, essential oils, or special scented candles.

Choose dried rose petals or collect your own, and float them with little round candles in dishes that will give a warm glow. Add essential oils to any water used to float the candles; it will give an overall scent to the room. You can even lightly drop oil onto large pillar candles when they are burning to fill the air with a special scent.

THIS PAGE:
Combine lanterns
and bowls to hold
floating candles.
Aim to stick to
natural materials
in neutral colors
before adding
brighter flowers
and petals.

OPPOSITE LEFT:
This delicate marble
bowl gives a soft
glow when the
candles are lit.

OPPOSITE RIGHT:
Tiny lanterns are
perfect to use
between bathrooms
and bedrooms.
Either float or stand
a candle inside.

BELOW: A wax vase gives a wonderful soft glow when lit with a floating candle.
RIGHT: This cozy bathroom is a haven of scent and soft light. Lanterns stand in a bucket of pebbles, and illuminated waxed paper cups sit on a ledge along the far wall.

Try customizing pots in which to put candles by wrapping interesting paper, such as Chinese paper or waxed gift wrap, around the outside. This can be quickly joined with clear tape and softens the light given out. Line up the holders along ledges, sills, or the edge of the tub.

In winter, when you're not using lanterns outdoors, hang them inside from crooks standing in buckets of sand or pebbles and shells.

Stick to soft lighting when relaxing in the bathroom and
bedroom. Look out for paper lanterns—even paper cups—
or attach soft-colored tissue paper to a glass lantern.

a gossamer-soft glow of scented candles

ABOVE: The bath rack holds all
the essentials for relaxation.
RIGHT: The near lantern has a
waxed paper cover, and the far
lantern is made from fabric. A
line of votives softly lights up the
window ledge when the loosely
woven linen curtains are drawn.

rare flowers

Pick up pretty one-off
candleholders and
candles when you see
them, and save them
for special bedroom
and bathroom moments.
Keep an eye out when
you are passing antique
stores and markets.

A decadent hanging candelabra or wall sconce can look very striking as the only source of light in a room. Consider replacing the candles in different colors to match your mood!

Floating candles come in many shapes and colors. Choose them in soft pastel colors and interesting shapes, and look out for flower-shaped candles that are especially effective floating individually in special bowls or as multiples in a row. You can float candles in practically any watertight container, as long as there is no danger of fire. Remember that the more opaque the vessel, the less light will shine through its walls.

OPPOSITE: A pretty antique candle sconce lights up this bedroom wall.
THIS PAGE: Flowerhead shapes are especially pretty in the bathroom and bedroom. These pretty white flowerhead candles have been brought out for a special, relaxing bathtime.

relish your relaxation

Indulge yourself in the bedroom with imposing candleholders for the simplest ivory wax pillars, or choose pretty colored candles and delicate glass-beaded holders.

The bedroom is the one room in the house where you can really indulge your decorative fantasies with candlelight. Whether you want to decorate your room with imposing pieces of classical architecture or plant towering flares beside your bed, hang romantic candelabra overhead or cover every surface with pretty pastel-colored gel candles, there's no excuse to hold back here. Look out for interesting holders in antique or thrift stores—even architectural salvage yards.

RIGHT: An interesting piece of architectural salvage has been recycled to hold altar candles in this fireplace. These will look great when all blazing together and will warm up this area of the bedroom.
CENTER: A floor-standing votive candle is perfect as a bedside light. This will give a soft light and is just the right height to be blown out at bedtime!
FAR RIGHT: A large hanging candelabra can light up the whole bedroom.

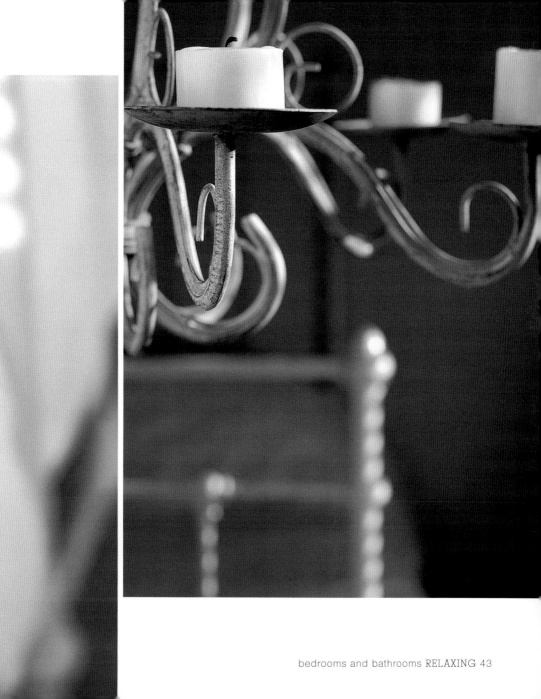

OPPOSITE:
Gel candles are
available in various
pastel shades. Try
grouping different
colors together.
THIS PAGE: Pretty
beaded holders add
a feminine touch to
the bedroom. These
are relatively cheap,
but look extremely
effective dotted
around the room.

EMBRACE CANDLELIGHT IN YOUR BEDROOM TO CREATE A SENSUAL DEN OF TRANQUILITY OR A FEAST OF EXOTIC COLOR

BELOW: This thick red pillar candle looks very effective within the dark metal of this decorative Indian lantern. Its golden glow will cast flickering shapes across the walls of the bedroom.

Be creative with lanterns around the home. Try casting moody light and shimmering shadows over your walls. Transform a bedroom with a decorative lantern that has shapes shrouding the candle flame to cast interesting shadows and patterns. Metal lanterns are particularly good for this effect. Also consider using colored glass lanterns, particularly North African and Indian styles, that will give an exotic feel to the bedroom. These look great when different colors and styles are used together in the same setting.

Freestanding lanterns can be placed on windowsills. It is worth looking at just how much light will penetrate into the room if the curtains are pulled across to hide it. A soft warm glow will be relaxing inside the room, and will look warm and welcoming from the outside to any visitors—but make absolutely sure that the curtains are not in danger of getting too close to the flame.

OPPOSITE: This is another Indian lantern, this time made from fabric with a metal spring inside so that it can be easily packed away and stored. It looks particularly good hanging on this antique bed frame.

THIS PAGE: These colored paper bags have been placed in a group in the undergrowth around the base of a tree. They would look equally eye-catching on a patio or balcony. Just pour in enough sand to support the candle, and make sure the flame is kept well away from the sides of the bag.

There is something very special about using candles outdoors. You don't have to wait for a calm summer's day to illuminate your backyard because there are plenty of ideas for slightly breezy days and cooler evenings.

Even a candle set at a relaxed alfresco lunch can be a treat—there doesn't have to be any practical excuse! There are, however, practical reasons, too: a line of lanterns will illuminate a dark path and citronella varieties help keep insects at bay during an early evening meal. Try to get hold of proper outdoor candles, which have thicker wicks—so they stay alight longer if a breezy patch comes along. They also often give out a brighter, stronger flame, which may be more suitable for practical purposes.

ILLUMINATING THE GARDEN

alfresco

ABOVE: Large hurricane lamps have been filled with colored liquid to float colored outdoor candles. Simply add a few drops of food coloring to the water—why not try this for a color-themed celebration?

THIS PAGE: Pebbles and thick red pillar candles surround a disposable barbecue. The red theme is taken up in all the lights, including a frosted-glass lantern and candles sitting in red galvanized-metal cones around the potted plant.

Illuminate your outdoor space with splashes of color. There's no need to stick to traditional backyard lighting. Improvise as much as possible and use nearby plant pots to support flares and holders.

hold a candle to nature

Choose a theme to work with and stick to it. Why not surround a barbecue with color and candlelight? Or use cone-shaped holders to nestle colorful candles among your plants. Colored paper bags make excellent holders, too; they look magical in groups or dotted randomly around the yard for a party. Hurricane lanterns are a more obvious choice for outdoors, but why not experiment with colored liquids and float candles inside for a change? Or collect pebbles from the beach to support a pillar candle.

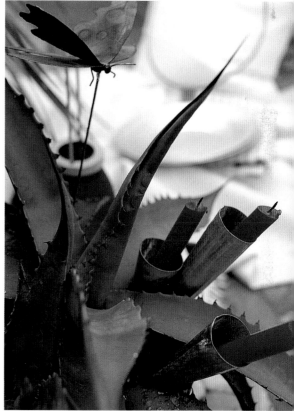

ABOVE AND LEFT: Bright-red candles look great against the rich green succulent and the soft tones of the pebbles.

A bright bowl of floating goodies!
This colorful lime-green candle
sits happily with the summer
flowerheads. Try picking flowers
from the garden—daisy and
dandelion heads are just as
effective, as long as everything
is kept bright and sunny!

Similar bowls of floating
flowers and candles have
been arranged at each
place setting on the deck in
preparation for a pretty lunch.

set planters and pots ablaze with light

Planters and pots make great homes for outdoor candles. Again, the secret is to improvise. Play around with flowerpots and seed trays, and "plant" candles in beds of tiny pebbles to keep them steady and the flame safe.

Use bags of fine pebbles, sand, and gravel to stand candles in trays. They are all available from decorative flower shops, garden centers and aquatic suppliers.

Tiny indoor greenhouses can also be transformed into interesting sources of light when they are not being used to propagate. The lid will also help keep the flames out of the breeze, so are good ideas for blustery days. And, if the weather turns out to be bad, make the most of any sheltered areas.

OPPOSITE LEFT:
A metal plant tray
makes a fitting
home for three large
outdoor candles set
in pebbles. Sitting
on the windowsill, it
will look good from
indoors or out.
OPPOSITE RIGHT:
Little galvanized
planters each hold
an outdoor floating
candle. Terracotta
would work just as
well. A piece of
slate makes an
interesting tray.
LEFT: Orderly rows
of tiny glass pots
holding little
candles fill this tray.

ABOVE: Any pot with a
punched-out pattern will look
delightful if it is illuminated.
RIGHT: These little Indian party
beakers are transformed into
tree lanterns by adding a wire
handle and a votive candle.
OPPOSITE LEFT: A small
terracotta pot has been adapted
to form an outside light.
OPPOSITE RIGHT: These cans
are filled with loose candle wax
around a long wick. It will burn
just as well as candles made by
the traditional method.

outdoor variety

Collect colorful containers to illuminate your backyard. You needn't buy specialized holders; just play with the basic glass jars and cans along ledges or hanging from the trees.

Vary your light sources by adapting holders into hanging lanterns— what could be more magical than an illuminated tree? As long as nothing can get burned or singed, suspend containers from handy branches. Simply punch holes in the side of tincans or wrap a length of wire around the top of a glass jar to attach a handle. Make a collection of colorful cans and fill them either with sand to support the stem of a candle or with a long central wick and grains or balls of candle wax to make your own.

ABOVE: Look out for interesting pieces that can double as candleholders. The bowl of an old birdbath provides the perfect dish for a group of wax pebble candles.
FAR LEFT: These pebble candleholders look great in multiples and are ideal to illuminate a garden pathway.
LEFT: Lanterns in different styles and colors look good arranged together in a line. The colored glass adds a special touch against the outdoor tones.

lighting the way

Candles can be more attractive than—and just as effective as—electrical lighting. Positioned along a path or at the steps to the front door, they will add interest and illumination to the arrival of an evening guest.

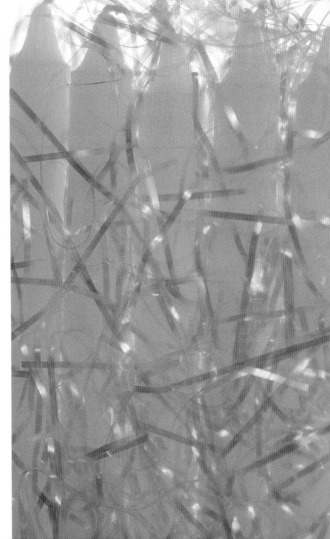

IDEAS TO MAKE AND GIVE
gifts

Candles make good gifts because you can never have too many! Even the simplest candles can make a beautiful and unusual gift when they are packaged with thought and care.

If you are giving an individual candle that will need an individual holder, why not wrap them both together? On the other hand, you can make your own candles as gifts. There are many simple candlemaking options available, and some don't require any heat at all. Just buy a complete candle wax that includes all necessary ingredients, and it will burn around a wick even in its original flaky state or in little balls of wax. Another option is a special gel that sets quickly to a jellylike consistency.

RIGHT: Plain candles make an excellent gift simply packaged in a clear envelope with a handful of iridescent cellophane strips.

BELOW: Candle gel must be heated to a certain state before it can be poured into a container to set. The beauty is that it can be built up in layers and other elements can be introduced in the making process. It is fun to experiment with decorative effects such as glitter.

all that glitters

Simple candles can be quickly made to look glamorous for a special occasion. Groups of glittering votives or candles made in sturdy colored glassware look dazzling at a party and make an unusual gift.

Try rolling plain solid wax candles in a shallow plateful of glitter—just the right amount will attach to the candle; there is no need for glue. You can also decorate the little metal cases around votives in a similar way: paint a layer of white glue around the outside, or simply attach a strip of double-sided tape and roll them in the glitter. And invest in some clear candle gel and a few heatproof colored glasses—you can make them again and again.

OPPOSITE: Votives encrusted in striking midnight-blue glitter look glorious when clustered together on a clear-glass plate— an inexpensive and innovative idea.

BELOW LEFT: A gel candle inside a little blue French-glass gives a beautiful colored glow.
BELOW: Long thin taper candles have been put in a clear plastic envelope to create an unusual gift.

A quick rummage in the kitchen cabinets will reveal a host of potential candleholders and molds you never knew you had! Invest in a candlemaking kit and start practicing.

get creative in the kitchen

ABOVE AND RIGHT: Brightly colored candle gel looks irresistible in metal molds and cookie cutters—perfect for a children's party and an exciting project for little people beforehand. Just keep small hands away from flames, and remember that they are not edible!

Small decorative food holders, such as pie pans and individual gelatin molds, are ideal containers in which to pour either liquefied candle gel or hot wax. The simpler kits provide ready-prepared wax or gel for the main body of the candle, plus the candle wicks. The wax or gel simply needs to be heated and then poured carefully around the wick before the candle is left to harden.

THIS PAGE: These candles in individual pie pans are ideal for each place setting at a birthday tea party. Though they won't last long, they can be recreated time and again. To make the event more fun, why not offer them from the baking tray?

ABOVE: This long rectangular candle is a place-setting gift for an outdoor evening meal, the idea being that each guest has their own candle to burn as the sun goes down. A piece of string secures a plant tag to personalize the gift.

a gift of rich red and brilliant metallics

The most basic of candles can be transformed into a special gift with the addition of a name tag or even just a piece of carefully tied ribbon.

Well-considered presentation, however simple, is the key to a beautifully packaged gift. Use these ideas for special little table gifts to put at individual settings; place them around the tree at Christmas for unexpected guests; or just hand them over with a card when you visit a friend.

Experiment with ribbon, metallic paper, cellophane, and little decorative envelopes for your candle gifts. Don't worry if you are pushed for time—just use your imagination: even a plain brown paper bag will make a good home for an altar candle when it is tied with green twine and personalized with an initialed luggage tag.

RIGHT: An unusual tincan is recycled to create a colorful coordinated gift.
LEFT: Little decorative Chinese envelopes make great homes for miniature candles. Why not make your own envelopes out of wrapping paper, magazine pages with interesting images, or foreign newspapers?

Candles can make relatively inexpensive tokens, so why not let a special wooden box or little organza ribbon-tied bag dictate your choice for the candle you give. It is the finishing touch that will make all the difference. Sit pretty floating candles in beds of soft bright feathers, or hide little beeswax cones in fabric purses. Wrap bright coordinating tissue paper around groups of plain colored standard candles and present them in bright bags. There's a candle gift idea for everyone!

You can take your gift ideas one step farther and find inspiration in your favorite fabrics or from unusual bags and boxes you have at home.

presents to set the party alight

ABOVE: Bright purple feathers liven up these silver boxes and make interesting beds for special candles. More feathers are attached to jewelry wire and wrapped around the boxes.
LEFT: Special beeswax candles sit in these richly colored organza bags.
RIGHT: A bright lime-green felted-wool bag has been lined with tissue paper and filled with coordinating candles.

STICK TO BRIGHT COLORS AND
INTERESTING TEXTURES, SUCH AS
ORGANZA, FEATHERS, AND TISSUE

LEFT: Special beeswax candles have been chosen as gifts and put into interesting wooden and metal boxes. RIGHT: A little metal tea box transforms a few votive candles into a precious gift. Jewelry wire is wrapped around the box to secure it, and a tiny brass bell adds a special finishing touch.

perfect packages

Look out for boxes in which to present candle gifts. The plainest vessel will do; then you can decorate it by adding your own details. Try wrapping wire around the box and adding beads, or attaching a little fabric flower to the end of a piece of ribbon. Old incense-stick envelopes and boxes are often a good length to reuse for candles.

An incense box is
recycled to hold
three fine beeswax
candles tied with
coordinating ribbon.
The colors—all
creams and
greens—look very
good together.

Entertaining is a good excuse to get out the candles! Rather than reach for those dusty ones that seem to hang around from occasion to occasion, give your candle treatment the same attention you give the food you serve.

You may be inspired by a color or a texture, a fabric or a paper. Decorative trimmings, for example, are a good starting point. They can be relatively inexpensive and are very effective wrapped around candles and holders. Feather trimming costs a little more, but the holders can be reused or given to guests at the end of the party (if they have gone down well!)

OPPOSITE: Feathers were the inspiration for the candle details on this table top. The orange, amber, and sage-green colors work very well together. Notice that the candles extend to the window ledge and will be dotted all around the room to carry the total theme.

BELOW: Feather trims have been attached with double-sided tape to the outsides of plain glasses.

FOR FAMILY AND FRIENDS

entertaining

Ideas that are inventive but simple are often the most successful. Sticking to a minimal palette of green, white, and natural wood gives a clean fresh look. Using glassware for the candleholders has further enhanced this, and the interaction with the large tropical leaves works well with the theme. Notice that the shot glasses stand on pieces cut from lush green leaves, reflected in the glass; and the water around the floating candles also magnifies the effect of leafy green color and texture.

This table has been laid in a cool modern style, built up in a series of layers using defined individual elements, and the candle details follow suit.

clean, modern, and minimal

RIGHT AND OPPOSITE: Each place has its own white candle supported by coarse salt in a shot glass. As the guests sit down, the candles can be put at the top of the place settings and lit. ABOVE: A big leaf has been cut to sit inside this glass cylinder. White pebbles support the leaf in the water, and a large floating candle finishes the look.

carving out a place

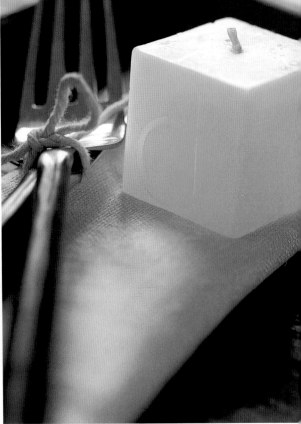

THIS PAGE: Flatware, napkins, and candles have been grouped on this tray for guests to pick out. Each candle has been initialed using a bamboo skewer or blunt pencil to carve out the letters—anything narrow and pointed will do.

To personalize a candle makes it a gift, and it could double up at the dining table as a way to guide guests to their seats instead of a placecard.

The waxy texture of candles makes it easy to carve an initial or a name in them. Candles can also be painted or written on; and the quickest way is to mark a name in indelible ink. Holders can be initialed, too—paint around the shape of a letter on a clear glass, for example. Alternatively, cut out an initial from a piece of paper and wrap it around a candle pot, or cut out letter shapes from a candle bag.

PERSONALIZED PLACE SETTINGS
OR GIFTS ALWAYS ADD A SPECIAL
TOUCH TO AN EVENT

SCOUR YOUR
CUPBOARDS FOR ANY
BRIGHTLY COLORED
GLASS DISHES AND
TUMBLERS

Candles look great in colorful holders. There are plenty of attractive glass, acrylic, and resin varieties available to buy.

a blaze of color and light for fun and festivity

It is often more fun to use glasses and bowls from your cabinets. Colored plastic glasses will also do, but secure the candle firmly to make sure the flame stays well away from the sides; it is advisable to stick the votive to the base of the glass or to secure it in a bed of sand.

ABOVE RIGHT: Moroccan tea glasses look very festive when lit up in a group. A box of six is relatively inexpensive, and you can use them again and again.
RIGHT: This unusual little light has a mesh of beaded wire surrounding a thick glass votive holder.
LEFT: Everyday glassware has been collected and recycled to be used as holders for an exotic display to give family and friends a warm welcome as they arrive.

A visit to the seaside inspired this candle display. The table has been laid with a rough sand-colored raffia runner as a background. Votive candles have been removed from their metal holders and placed in beds of tiny pebbles. Pebble candleholders also feature, holding both votives and taller candles, and little oyster shells have been recycled to hold seasoning at each setting and to burn with wax gel along the center of the table.

BELOW: Transfers can be fun, and there are plenty of designs and colors to choose from. These altar candles have been given transfers similar to henna tattoos and would make a lovely gift either individually or as a set of three. They sit very well here among the ethnic decoration on the mantelpiece.

Never mind the holders—you can decorate the candles themselves
to create individual and unusual gifts or as another way to extend
a decorative theme when you are entertaining at home.

decorative detailing

Decorate candles with paint, stickers, or transfers—there
are plenty of popular tattoo-style transfers available in
jewelry and cosmetic stores. Make sure you start with
clean unmarked candles and decorate as you desire. You
can also apply bindis—traditional Indian face decorations.
They are often bright and glittery, and perfect for parties.
Another alternative, particularly good if you are entertaining
with a metallic theme, is gold and silver leaf. It attaches to
a waxy surface easily and looks glamorous and decadent.

RIGHT: Squares
of silver and gold
leaf have been
applied to one side
of each cube candle.
LEFT: A votive
candle has been
removed from its
metal holder and
decorated with a
ring of bindis.

the rough with the smooth

As we have seen, candles come in every color, shape and size. Texture is just another interesting theme to explore when creating themed occasions.

There are numerous surface textures available, and candles can be found that simulate concrete, pebbles, stone, and many other materials. It is also fun to mix textured candles with other textured elements, such as sand, gravel, and glass gravel (gravellike pieces of recycled glass, often available from florists as a decorative treatment). Look out for stonelike candleholders and dishes that can be used in your candle displays. Other natural elements such as slate and wood make a good base for a display built on texture.

RIGHT: This spherical candle has a grooved surface that works well with the recycled piece of slate beneath. CENTER: Candles with interesting textures have been laid out along a long wooden bench ready to be set for a buffet. The slabs of slate act as "placemats" for each candle display.

BELOW: Make a feature of the elements surrounding your candles. These two cube candles have smooth flat surfaces that look great juxtaposed against the iridescence of the glass gravel around them. The color of the slate brings out the texture and light in the display.

THIS PAGE: Natural and toffee-colored wax looks great with white china and plain linen napkins against the dark wooden furniture in this beach house. A few oak leaves have been added to complete the setting.

RIGHT: These wax balls have been bought complete with wicks in cellophane bags. Simply cut the wick to the required length and hold it centrally over a dish, then pour in the balls.

pantry inspirations

It is well worth keeping a stash of candlemaking elements in your home. Impromptu but interesting candles can then be made in a flash, should the mood take you or if unexpected guests pop in.

Your candlemaking materials could include wax gel, wicks, and solid wax in either flakes, grains, or larger balls. The beauty of these elements is that they can be assembled in almost any sort of container, as long as it is not flammable. If you are on vacation and only have basic kitchen elements on hand, there will most likely be suitable heat-resistant bowls and glasses there. Improvise with recycled plant pots, tincans, and glass jars, too. Stick to a natural palette for the wax colors, and they will look great with basic white china and glassware.

ABOVE RIGHT: Improvise with the elements around you. A little metal saucer that usually sits under a potted plant has been made into a candleholder by the simple addition of wax balls and a wick.

candles
FOR SPECIAL OCCASIONS

Every occasion can be a special occasion, whether it is a traditional celebration such as Christmas or New Year, a child's party, or simply a quiet evening at home with a loved one. Inspiration can come from any source: an abundance of harvest fare at Thanksgiving; feathers and eggs at Easter; or purely from the colors and textures of the candles you are using. Whatever your starting point, the theme and style of your illumination should be remembered, so go ahead and enjoy yourself!

Celebrate an icy New Year with seasonal red berries and pure white taper candles. Use sparkling glass to bring out the coolness of the white candles and the brightness of the red berries.

When working to a theme, arrange the candle decorations around the home so that guests will see them the moment they step through your door. If there are no candles outside, make sure there is a welcoming glow at the window. Even if your curtains are closed, a storm lantern can sit happily and safely on the ledge to beckon guests inside.

ICY COOL CHIC
new year

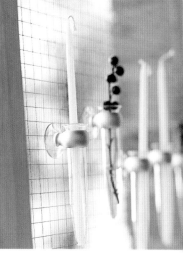

ABOVE: Suction vases cling to the windows, complementing the minimal style of the apartment. LEFT: This dip tray houses a bright-white wax floating flower alongside a dish of freshly cut slices of lime for cocktails.

icy cool chic NEW YEAR 91

THIS PAGE: Glass, glass, and more glass brings a delicate icy quality to the decoration. The bases of these candlesticks are hollow and ideal for this unusual decorative trick where the berries sit inside.

LEFT: These pebble holders can be used with or without the glass tubes.
BELOW: Coarsely ground sea salt sits alongside candles in a tray that looks as if it has been carved from a block of ice.

Make sure glassware is sparkling clean, and alternate winter berries with glowing flames. Test-tube vases are particularly good for this effect. Look out for runs of test tubes or tubes with a suction pad to stick to windows, mirrors, or tiles—some tubes can be bought sitting in pebbles, too. Though these vases are primarily for flowers, they make a good rest for a candle. Just don't let the flame burn too low.

THIS PAGE: This welcoming table is laden with richly colored food and illumination. A green bamboo tray holds a decorative host of thick pillar candles and gourds, even faux-bamboo candles that match the tray. Fall shades of green, red, and orange predominate.
RIGHT: A colored glass holds a floating candle. The flame gives a lovely warm reflection.

RIGHT: A little group of colored beeswax taper candles tied with a scrap of fabric, brown paper, and metallic thread makes the perfect table gift.

Warm shades of orange, amber, and green prevail in an abundance of harvest vegetables and a riot of rich natural color. Use your creative skills to the full.

Choose coordinating candles in thick pillar styles, and team them with little candleholders in the same palette. Use similarly colored glassware and warm-toned rustic china for the table setting.

Wrap the bases of thick candles in leaves and secure them with grass or string ties. Support smaller candles in little pots of dried peas and beans and float candles in brightly colored glasses. Potatoes or turnips also make

thanksgiving

FIERY FALL FARE

AIM FOR A LOOK TO RADIATE WARMTH AND WELCOME

ideal candleholders. Simply cut a suitable hole in each root vegetable and add a candle—an unusual and humorous touch! They look great in a wonky row along the center of a table or across a mantelpiece or window ledge. And why not give each guest their own holder to take home?

Remember to extend the candle details beyond the main table setting and continue the theme around your home. Light everything early, to make sure guests are greeted with a warm glow in the hall and flickering light at the windows.

OPPOSITE: Layer your ideas: groups of tiny beeswax tapers stand in glass pots of dried beans that sit amid little chile peppers on wooden saucers.
LEFT: Textured green cabbage leaves have been wrapped around the bases of wide pillar candles and tied tightly with thick strands of grass.
ABOVE: Imaginative and inexpensive candleholders! A row of potatoes runs along the center of a table setting. Gourds or turnips would be just as effective.

Don't confine birthday candles to the cake! Instead, add to the general glitter and sparkle of the event by displaying them all around the room.

Unless you have a specific decorative theme, choose a couple of bright colors and stick to that palette. If you are working to a budget, use plain white china and simple glassware, and invest in a good stock of basic votive candles as a starting point. The glass will reflect flames, and plain china will accentuate any bright colors. Look out for inexpensive coordinating

LEFT: These tapers have been cunningly propped with glass rings that are normally used to support flowerheads in water. OPPOSITE AND BELOW: The glass table top and little tin candleholders sparkle, and, along with shiny plates, make way for the bright decorations.

SPARKLING REFLECTIONS
birthday

THIS PAGE: Layer your glassware for maximum decorative effect. A cylindrical vase sits in a large tall vase, leaving enough room for an unusual ring of bright feathers. The long taper candles are supported in a cluster of clear glass balls.

OPPOSITE LEFT: A few bright sequins have been added to the water in this bowl to cast pretty spots of color.

BRIGHT COLORS, REFLECTIVE GLASS, AND FLICKERING FLAMES MAKE A SPECIAL SETTING

decorations such as feathers, ribbons, and sequins. Drop a few sequins into vases of water with floating candles. Stand plain bright candles in cups of glass gravel. Put out table gifts—a simple candle tied with brightly colored ribbon and a feather will look great at each setting. Also, rummage through your Christmas decorations: they needn't be confined to Christmas, so search for plain glass or glitter balls, and see if they will fit in with your birthday theme.

BELOW: These holders stick to tiles, windows, or walls. Keep a stock of votive candles and refill as necessary.

OPPOSITE: A bright gingham cloth makes the perfect backdrop to colorful settings. Little pots have been stacked here, but unstack them before lighting the candles so that sweet-seeking fingers don't get burned. RIGHT: These candles are safely out of little hands' reach. Experiment with colored liquids, food coloring, and other decorations to build up interesting layers. BELOW: Cake pans and cookie cutters come to the fore!

BRIGHT LIGHTS

kid's party

When it comes to children's parties, there is no need to stick to the conventional. As long as your ideas are safe and effective, anything goes!

Children's parties are so exciting! You can use candles at a children's party if the guests and birthday child are old enough to know and understand that fire should not be played with, and adult supervision must be constant. Your decorations will depend on the age of your young guests. Floating candles or candles in holders within larger holders are often best for younger ages. The advantage of using

THIS PAGE: A tray of individual pies waits to be brought out. Soon everyone will have a candle to blow out and a wish to make.
RIGHT: All these candles coordinate with the crayons, candy, and party setting as a whole, including the row of bright gerbera in the background. Once again, the plain glassware enhances surrounding colors.

floating candles is that you can adjust the water level to keep them out of reach. There is nothing to stop you from floating other items in the water, too.

You can add to these with candles in plain bright colors. Choose sturdy little pillar candles and round floating candles, and buy a few coordinating flowers.

Whatever happens, don't forget the cake. There is a wide variety of cake candles to choose from, including long-burning and miniature-sparkler varieties, as well as a good range of colors. If you don't want to follow the conventional route, buy or bake individual cakes and pop a candle into each one.

Valentine's day—the perfect excuse to start a fire! Create just the right amount of illumination for an evening of romance, and who knows what might happen ...

Reds and pinks are an obvious choice for this occasion. Remember that there are plenty of ways to accentuate a color scheme. Floating candles can be immersed in colored liquid; lanterns and candleholders are available in many different shades; or use your imagination and wrap clear glass vessels or lanterns in red cellophane.

RIGHT: Unusual black flower-shaped floating candles fill these little holders, and a decorative heart sticker gives a special touch.
LEFT: Create a romantic haven with different heights of light to give just the right glow.

valentine

SOFT FLAMES AND HOT COLORS

THIS PAGE: A red glass dish
glows romantically with the
addition of a couple of candles.
A few rose petals have been
added to the water to go with
the overall theme.

FAR LEFT: A line of glass candle pots runs along the beam. Food coloring has been added to the water, and a tiny candle has been put in each one. Light them just as your special guest arrives; they won't burn long, but they look great while they do! LEFT: A slightly different take on teaming candles with flowerheads. Keep the stems on these tall roses and they will look great standing alongside the lantern crook, steadied in a vase full of big pebbles and water.

halloween

Gather fallen leaves and collect gourds and squash for

a welcoming display that is more sparkling than spooky!

Lay candles on big colorful leaves before they dry out. There has been a long tradition of carving pumpkins, but you do not have to stick to the traditional pumpkin face; try carving patterns in the skin and see the play of light through the different shapes. Even a quick band of circles removed with an apple corer will be effective. Gourds,

THIS PAGE: Candlelit pumpkins look radiant on a bed of fall leaves or grouped together. Store carved pumpkins in the cool when not in use, and they will last a long time.

CHOCOLATE EGGS AND FEATHER NESTS
easter

Easter may not be the most obvious occasion for candles, but an unexpected candlelit feast of chocolate eggs is guaranteed to bring sparkle and excitement to the day!

Nests and eggs are the main ingredients of an Easter theme, and although candles are not naturally associated with chocolate eggs, they work well together as long as they don't get too close to each other! Have fun and search for egg-shaped and basic round candles that will sit happily in pretty eggcups. Arm yourself with some inexpensive clear glass or plastic eggcups and a pack

OPPOSITE: Even the candle in the storm lantern sits on a bed of pretty miniature foil-wrapped eggs. The eggs will be gone long before the pillar burns down and melts them! RIGHT: Decorate glassware to create unusual candleholders. This pretty holder has been made from a plain glass with the addition of soft purple feathers.

ABOVE: A plain spherical candle sits in a delicate wire holder. Eggcups themselves can also double as holders.

LEFT: These peacock feathers look effective when strung around the outside of a chunky plain glass vase. A variety of other basic vessels, such as glass tumblers and votive holders, are given the same treatment.

AN ECLECTIC MIX OF DELICATE
FEATHERS AND PRETTY FOIL
FOLLOWS A SOFT COLOR PALETTE

of candlemaking gel, and make a few extra inedible Easter gifts for your guests to enjoy. These will be a little surprise laid at each place setting.

Once again, choose a color scheme carefully. You may prefer to stick to plain neutral candles and bring out your chosen palette in the candle details and their decoration. A variety of bright feathers attached around the outside of a selection of glass candle pots, and a scattering of colored sequins added to some candle gel, will soon bring color to your display.

LEFT: Basic clear glass eggcups make inexpensive and reusable candleholders. The suspended sequins in this homemade gel candle give it a special touch—a perfect little table gift.

The holidays are an ideal opportunity to use candles in the home. Choose styles to match your chosen theme and place them in the fireplace, on the mantelpiece, on windowsills, and across the table.

Decorate a table with brilliant white candles that have been rolled over a bed of silver glitter. They won't need any glue to attract just the right amount of sparkle. Choose everyday kitchenware—clear glass pots and bright white dishes—to hold the candles, and set them on festive leaves such as holly and ivy for an inexpensive but effective display.

BELOW LEFT: Small pure white candles have been decorated with glitter and placed in little glass pots standing on leaves to form a decorative trail across the middle of the table.
BELOW: Elegant taper candles standing in a tall glass add height to the overall Christmas table setting.
RIGHT: A glittery pillar candle sits on a bed of winter leaves in a special star-shaped dish.

FIRE, ICE, AND SNOW

holiday

LEFT: Fun bangles add a touch of festive sparkle, and strips of metallic tape are wound around the base of a colored glass. BELOW LEFT: Everything is sparkling and reflective. A general dusting of sequins finishes off the scene. RIGHT: Chinese paper decorates a wide pillar candle—squares of gold leaf on a strip of baking parchment will give a similar effect.

DAZZLING AND EXOTIC
holiday

Mix warm tones of orange, red, and pink to bring an exotic feel to the festive season. Rummage through your old decorations and pull out anything that fits the theme.

It is always worth buying a few extra sequins, lengths of ribbon, and so on, so you can decorate the candles themselves if you need more sparkle and color. So long as they don't come in contact with the flame, candle decorations can be made from any material. Inexpensive jewelry and bangle bracelets make unusual additions. Beads and buttons, too, can be attached to wire and wound around the base of a candle.

holiday

Who can resist the charm of a traditional Christmas? Shades of red, green, and gold prevail, and deep-orange candle flames enhance the festive feel.

Decorate candleholders with holly and ivy both inside and out. Large hurricane lamps are ideal since they leave you lots of room to wind foliage around the base of a candle.

Remember to spread your candle details around your home and aim for versatility. A good idea is to create displays that can be easily moved around, such as a welcoming decoration on a side table in the hall that later becomes a centerpiece on the dining table.

TOP LEFT: A ring of wire mesh has been pulled over a basic altar candle. LEFT AND FAR LEFT: Pretty Christmas candles can be displayed with other decorations, such as beaded fruit and plain-colored glass balls.

ABOVE: A basic wire urn has been simply but carefully decorated with ivy and little birds. A large brown candle sits inside on a bed of foil-covered chocolate coins. It will also look wonderful as a centerpiece at holiday dinner.

STOCKISTS AND SUPPLIERS

ABC CARPET & HOME
For a store near you,
call (561) 279-7777
www.abchome.com
Furniture, furnishings, and accessories.

AD HOC SOFTWARES
136 Wooster Street
New York, NY 10012
(212) 982-7703
Interesting homeware and accessories.

ANTHROPOLOGIE
375 West Broadway
New York, NY 10012
For a store near you,
call (212) 343-7070
www.anthropologie.com
Reproduction decorative hardware,
including glass lanterns.

APARTMENT 48
48 West 17th Street
New York, NY 10011
(212) 807-1391
New and antique home furnishings.

BED BATH & BEYOND
620 Avenue of the Americas
New York, NY 10011
(212) 255-3550
Superstore with home accessories,
including candles.

CANDLECHEM COMPANY
56 Intervale Street
Brockton, MA 02302
(508) 586-1880
www.alcasoft.com/candlechem

Candle-making products: scents, dyes,
pigments, wax additives, molds, waxes,
and beeswax sheets.

THE CANDLE SHOP
118 Christopher Street
New York, NY 10014
(888) 823-4823
www.candlexpress.com

CANDLESHTICK
2444 Broadway
New York, NY 10024
(212) 787-5444

CAROLINA CANDLE COMPANY
6831 US Highway 311
Sophia, NC
(800) 388-6299
www.carolinacandlecompany.com
Specialize in highly scented candles.

CHANDLERS CANDLE COMPANY
(800) 463-7143
www.chandlerscandle.com
Hand-crafted and personalized candles.

COLONIAL CANDLE OF CAPE COD
232 Main Street
Hyannis, MA 02601
(800) 437-1238 for mail order
Well-known manufacturer of pillars,
tapers, and classic candles.

THE CONRAN SHOP
407 East 59th Street
New York, NY 10022
(212) 755-9079
www.conran.com

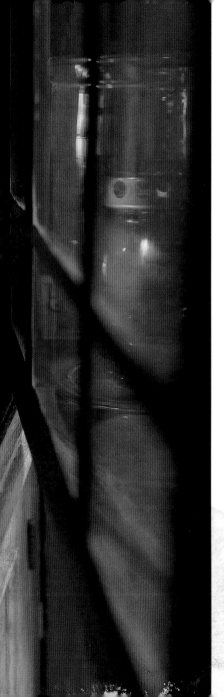

COVINGTON CANDLE

976 Lexington Avenue
New York, NY 10021
(212) 472-1131
Custom-made dinner and pillar candles
in a good range of colors and sizes.

CRATE & BARREL

1860 West Jefferson Avenue
Naperville, IL 60540
For a store near you,
call (800) 927-9202
www.crateandbarrel.com
Dinnerware, furniture, and accessories,
including candles and holders.

CREATIVE CANDLES

P.O. Box 412514
Kansas City, MO 64141
(800) 237-9711
www.creativecandles.com
Specializes in hand-dipped tapers,
pillars, and spheres in 47 colors.

ECLECTIC HOME

224 Eighth Avenue
New York, NY 10011
(212) 225-2373
Colorful, funky furniture, lighting,
glassware, housewares, and candles.

ENCHANTED CANDLE

22 Greenwich Avenue
New York, NY 10014
(212) 924-1101

ENFLEURAGE

321 Bleecker Street
New York, NY 10014
(212) 691-1610
www.enfleurage.com
Candles, oils, and soaps.

FLIGHTS OF FANCY

1502 First Avenue
New York, NY 10021
(212) 772-1302
Candles and decorative items.

GALILEO

37 Seventh Avenue South
New York, NY 10014
(212) 243-1629
Great vintage and new furniture,
tableware, linens, candles, and
decorative items.

GLOBAL TABLE

107–109 Sullivan Street
New York, NY 10012
(212) 431-5839
www.globaltable.com
Wonderful collection of tableware and
glassware, plus unusual candles.

GUMP'S

135 Post Street
San Francisco, CA 94108
(415) 982-1616
www.gumpsbymail.com
Homewares and accessories.

HUDSON DRY GOODS

873 Broadway
New York, NY 10003
For a store near you,
call (212) 228-7143

ILLUMINATIONS

1995 South McDowell Boulevard
Petaluma, CA 94954
800-CANDLES (226-3537)
www.illuminations.com
An array of candles, candle
accessories, and home-decor products.

JAMSONS
316 Bleecker Street
New York, NY 10014
(212) 255-6420
Mostly bamboo items, some furniture,
great candles, carved wood, terracotta.

LL BEAN
95 Main Street
Freeport, ME 04032-9967
(800) 453-0340
www.llbean.com
Outdoor accessories, including
candles and lanterns.

MAISON D'ETRE
92 South Park
San Francisco, CA 94107
(415) 357-1747
www.maisondetre.com

MXYPLYZYK
125 Greenwich Avenue
New York, NY 10014
(212) 989-4300
Up-to-the-minute furniture and
decorative items.

NICE HOUSE
117 Perry Street
New York, NY 10014
(212) 675-7509
Vintage 1940s–70s furnishings,
including candlesticks, plus new
candles and storage boxes.

NORTHERN LIGHTS CANDLES
3474 Andover Road
Wellsville, NY 14895
(716) 593-1200
www.northernlightscandles.com
Candles of all varieties.

**PEARL RIVER CHINESE
PRODUCTS**
277 Canal Street
New York, NY 10013
(212) 219-8107
Fashion and home accessories.

PIER 1 IMPORTS
499 Tarrytown Road
White Plains, NY 10607
For a store near you,
call (800) 44-PIER1
www.pier1.com
Big selection of candles, holders,
dinnerware, and accessories.

PORTICO
72 Spring Street
New York, NY 10012
(212) 941-7800
Shaker-style furniture and accessories.

POTTERY BARN
For a store near you,
call (800) 922-9934
www.potterybarn.com
Furniture and accessories, including
candles, holders, and lanterns.

POURETTE
(800) 888-9425 for mail order
www.pourette.com
A complete selection of candle-making
supplies, such as beeswax sheets, wax
beads, block wax, molds, and wicks.

RESTORATION HARDWARE
For a store near you,
call (800) 816-0969
www.restorationhardware.com
Furnishings and accessories, including
a range of candles and holders.

TABULA TUA
1015 West Armitage
Chicago, IL 60614
(773) 525-3500
www.tabulatua.com

TERRA COTTA
259 West Fourth Street
New York, NY 10014
(212) 243-1952
Artisan home accessories.

WILLIAMS-SONOMA
51 Highland Park Village
Dallas Highland
Dallas, TX 75205
For a store near you,
call (800) 541-2233
www.williamssonoma.com
Kitchenware, candles, and holders.

YANKEE CANDLE CO.
South Deerfield, MA 01373
For a retailer near you,
call (877) 803-6890
www.yankeecandle.com
Scented candles.

PICTURE CREDITS

The author and publisher would like to
thank the following people for allowing
us to photograph their homes or their
work: Ros Badger; Janet Chalmers;
Clare Mannix-Andrews; Lewis Rowe;
Jo Saker; Robert Shackleton; TAG
Architects, Architecture & Interior Design,
14 Belsize Crescent, London NW3 5QU,
UK (44) 20 7431 7974; Susie Wilson.

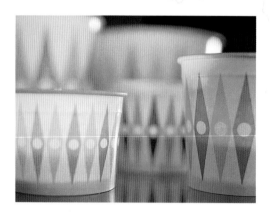

acknowledgments

Thank you to David for his enthusiasm and dedication—a very
special individual. Thanks also to Catherine, Mark, and Sophie for
completing the creative team.
A huge thankyou goes to all the family and friends who let us into
their beautiful homes, and finally thanks once again to the talented team
at Ryland Peters & Small for the chance to produce this book.